This book belongs to

_____

# HOLIDAYS AROUND THE WORLD

A Bantam  Book

BANTAM BOOKS

TORONTO • NEW YORK • LONDON • SYDNEY • AUCKLAND

RL 3, 4–8

HOLIDAYS AROUND THE WORLD
*A Bantam Book / May 1986*

*PRINTING HISTORY*

*Adapted from the Walt Disney Fun-to-Learn Library:*
It's a Small World *(volume 12) and*
Seasons and Holidays *(volume 13).*

**Library of Congress Cataloging-in-Publication Data**
Main entry under title:

Holidays around the world.

(A Bantam begin-to-learn book)
Summary: The Disney characters introduce holidays
from all over the world.
1. Holidays—Juvenile literature. [1. Holidays]
I. Series.
GT3933.H65  1986      394.2'6      85–22955
ISBN 0-553-05416-3

*Published simultaneously in the United States and Canada*

---

*Bantam Books are published by Bantam Books, Inc. Its trade-*
*mark, consisting of the words "Bantam Books" and the por-*
*trayal of a rooster, is Registered in U.S. Patent and Trademark*
*Office and in other countries. Marca Registrada. Bantam*
*Books, Inc., 666 Fifth Avenue, New York, New York 10103.*

---

PRINTED IN THE UNITED STATES OF AMERICA

0 9 8 7 6 5 4 3 2 1

Classic® binding, R. R. Donnelley & Sons Company. U.S. Patent
No. 4,408,780; Patented in Canada 1984; Patents in other
countries issued or pending.

# IT'S A SMALL WORLD

Today is It's-a-Small-World Day at Morty and Ferdie's
school. Everyone is very excited. The children are going to taste
foods from other lands and learn lively folk dances. They'll
even get to try on some costumes.

Best of all, Mickey is there! Mickey has been around the world many times and has visited children from every land. He is going to tell the children about the countries he has visited and show them some of his pictures.

IT'S -A-
SMALL-WORLD DAY

Yvette and her friend Mark live in Canada. They love to go ice fishing in the long, cold winter.

Each year, they help Yvette's parents drag a little wooden cabin out onto the frozen river. A fire helps to keep the cabin warm inside. Then the two friends make a hole in the ice through an opening in the cabin floor. They bait their hooks and wait for the fish to bite.

"Come inside," calls Yvette. "It's much more fun in here."

It's a very, very merry Christmas in Mexico. Carlos and Alicia are going to break a piñata with their friends. A piñata is a big, hollow toy filled with candy and little toys and fruit all wrapped up in brightly colored paper.

The guests take turns trying to break open the piñata with a stick until—*smack,* out fall the goodies.

Astrud and Roberto live in Rio de Janeiro, a city in Brazil. At carnival time, there is no other place they would rather be. For one full week during the Brazilian summer, the schools and shops close so that everyone can go to parties and dances. The streets are decorated with flowers, and special bands come to the city to play Brazilian tunes called sambas.

What are Rosita and Paco doing with all those paper bags
full of balloons? They are getting ready for carnival time in Peru.
They have brought brightly colored powders to mix with water.
Then they will fill each balloon with a different-colored water.

Rosita and Paco join in the biggest water fight ever.
Even mothers and fathers enjoy the fun. It looks
as though the children have found the best
place to shower their friends with color.
*Splash, splash!* Soon everyone in town
will look like a gaily colored Easter egg.

In winter, Norway is a land of beautiful snowy mountains. Almost everyone in Norway knows how to ski. Kirsten learned to ski when she was only three years old. Other children might slide down the mountain the way Anders does, on a round piece of metal that looks like a pie plate.

Imagine walking in the middle of the night to see the sun shining! In Norway, the summer sun shines almost as brightly at midnight as it does at midday! That is why Norway is called the Land of the Midnight Sun.

Anders and Kirsten stay up all night to celebrate the first day of summer. The children stack all the wood and paper they can find in great big piles. Then, at the stroke of midnight, their parents set the piles on fire. Everyone cheers. Summer is here!

Tommy and Jill live in London, England's capital city. In London, stories about kings and queens, princes and princesses, and horses and palace guards come true! Today, Tommy and Jill have joined the crowd outside Buckingham Palace, the home of the queen. A grand procession is just starting out through the palace gates.

The palace guards
wear splendid uniforms
with tall, furry hats.
Their faces are very
serious.

Paris is the capital city of France and
one of the prettiest cities in the world. Perhaps this is
why so many artists have chosen to live there. Mickey is
having his picture painted by one of them now. It looks as though
Goofy could use a few lessons.

Gilbert and Marie have just been to the bakery to buy breakfast.
Those special long loaves of bread that they are carrying are called
*baguettes*. The children are going to share their fresh-baked bread
with Mickey and Goofy.

*Kindergarten* is a German word meaning "garden of children." For Hans and Greta, the first day of school is a happy one. Each of them gets a giant cone filled with candy to sweeten the day. How handsome they look, wearing their brand-new school clothes.

"Smile, please," says Donald. Poor Dewey thought he was getting a new hat!

Instead of fairy tales, Greek
children love to hear stories about their
favorite gods, goddesses, and ancient
heroes. The make-believe gods could
make thunder when they were angry and
rainbows when they were glad. Morty
and Ferdie think that Goofy would make
a great Greek hero, but Mickey is not so
sure.

Nick and Ana each have a donkey to take them up the narrow mountain trails around their village in Greece. Huey and Dewey are having fun—but whatever happened to Donald?

The Festival of the Crickets is a great favorite of Maria and Dominic of Italy. To celebrate spring, the children buy a cricket and a miniature cage for it. Maria and Dominic take good care of their new little friend. They feed it bits of lettuce and listen to it sing.

At the end of the day, they set it free.

Abram and Ruth of Israel live on a kibbutz. This is a big farm where many mothers and fathers and their children live together. Each person helps with the job he or she does best. And with so many people at the table, dinnertime is always fun.

Afterward, everyone helps do the dishes.

Today, all the schoolchildren will dress up in costumes. They will go to a carnival where they will sing and dance. This is how Jewish children celebrate Purim, the feast of the great queen Esther.

Fatima and Omar of Egypt sleep in a tent beneath the stars every night. Because the desert is so dry, they take their tent, goats, and camels with them from place to place in search of water.

Tonight they are sleeping near the Great Pyramids. Those huge buildings are the tombs where three famous kings, or pharaohs, of Egypt were buried—long, long ago. And there, crouching in the sand, is the mighty Sphinx. This huge statue, with the head of a human and the body of a lion, is guarding the Pyramids from all who would harm them.

For Togbi and Kofi of Ghana, today is a very special day. The whole village will celebrate because the people are getting a new chief. Here comes the parade now!

Togbi and Kofi's father, the new chief, is being carried in a grand procession through the village. The colorful umbrellas whirl and twirl to the rhythm of the drums. How proud the children must feel.

No, Goofy, it isn't raining. The umbrellas shade the chief from the blazing-hot sun.

Ilunga of Zaire can't wait to be thirteen years old. For only then will he be old enough to wear one of the wonderful masks of his tribe. There are ugly masks to frighten away evil spirits and happy ones to wear at celebrations. Some masks are the faces of animals.

Krishna and Chandra of India have left their tiny village to explore the city for a day.

There's so much for them to see! The women look lovely as they walk down the street in graceful saris. By the curb, camels share parking spaces with cars. And on a corner, Krishna and Chandra notice some pretty things to buy. How grown-up they feel as they choose presents to take home for their mother.

When Krishna and Chandra return to their village, still more excitement awaits them. A special autumn festival will brighten the village. There will be puppet shows and parades. Everyone will wear their finest clothes. The elephants will even have their toenails polished and wear colorful designs painted on their trunks and sides.

In Moscow, the capital city of the Soviet Union, there is a special school for children who want to become circus performers. Here, Natasha learns the trapeze, wire walking, and acrobatics, as well as reading and arithmetic.

If she becomes a bear trainer, she will travel all over the world with Boris, the bear, and the famous Moscow Circus. Take a bow, Natasha. Perhaps someday you will be the star of the show.

Mischa thinks Leningrad is the most beautiful city in the Soviet Union. He loves to show off its palaces, statues, and fountains. His favorite place is the children's park at Peterhof. It's a wonderland, with magic fountains that spring up right beneath your feet when you least expect them.

Mei Chu and Kwang Ling live in the People's Republic of China, the country with the largest number of people in the world.

Imagine the excitement as so many people celebrate holidays together. For Mei Chu and Kwang Ling, the New Year is the happiest time of all, because the holiday lasts for several days.

This is the evening of the Lantern Festival. On this last
day of the New Year celebrations, huge lions parade through
the streets. The children wave paper flowers and scatter confetti.
Red envelopes with money are hung in doorways for good luck.
And all around, firecrackers hiss and explode in the air.

In Japan, little girls love dolls so much that they have a special Doll's Day every year to honor them. Today, Yasuko has some new dolls to add to her collection. Of course, the emperor and empress dolls will go on the top shelf because they are the fanciest.

Yasuko's friends arrive for her party looking like beautiful butterflies in their favorite kimonos. She serves them delicious rice cakes she has prepared herself.

Then they will visit the homes of other friends to admire their dolls and to eat their special food.

On Boy's Day
in Japan, you can see fish
swimming in the sky! They're
not real fish, of course, but beautifully colored
kites that are shaped like fish.

Yoji has worked for days to make a perfect
kite. It is hollow, so the wind will fill it up.
And he has used such brightly colored paper
that all his friends will see his kite in the
Boy's Day parade.

Steve and his friend Christy live in New York City, the city with the most people in the United States of America. Whenever the children have visitors, they like to take them to the Statue of Liberty. This huge statue holds her torch high to welcome all who visit her. From the top of her crown, you will have a wonderful view of one of the most famous skylines in the world—that of New York City.

Did you ever pretend you were a cowboy or a cowgirl? That's what Bob and Susanna want to be when they grow up. They live on a cattle ranch in Oklahoma, so they get plenty of practice riding and roping. They'll show off what they can do at the rodeo today. Here comes Goofy on a bucking bronco—how long do you think he can stay on?

The children at Morty and Ferdie's school agree that there's one thing children all over the world like to do—they like to have fun!

All the children want to thank Mickey for helping them celebrate their special day.

In Japan, children say *arigato* for "thank you."
Mexican children say *gracias*.
Norwegian children say *takk*.
In Israel, children say *toda*.
French children say *merci*.
And to all the children, Mickey says, "Thank *you*, everyone, thank *you*."

# SEASONS AND HOLIDAYS

There are some days that you know are going to be special even before you get out of bed. "Today is different," you say to yourself. "It's a holiday and something wonderful is going to happen!"

But what is a holiday? It is a special day set aside for rest or play or for remembering something important or someone great.

Each season has its own holidays for us to look forward to. Every holiday has its own customs that make it special.

Join Mickey and his friends as they take you through a year filled with holidays we can all celebrate together. Have fun!

It's New Year's Eve and Mickey is having a party. Minnie, Morty, and Ferdie are helping Mickey get ready. Morty and Ferdie are very excited because this is one night that they are allowed to stay up late.

Morty is making funny paper hats for the guests to wear. Ferdie is cutting colored paper into tiny pieces for confetti. When the clock strikes midnight, they will throw the confetti into the air to welcome the New Year.

"Look at the clock," cries Mickey. "Let's get out the noisemakers!"

"Ten, nine, eight, seven, six, five, four, three, two, one!"

Everyone counts backward together.

"The New Year is here!" Minnie announces.

"Happy New Year!" cry Morty and Ferdie.

On Saint Valentine's Day, it's fun to tell people how much we like them. This custom started a long time ago in Rome. The Roman people used to think that there was a god named Cupid, a chubby little fellow with wings.

According to the old Roman stories, Cupid would fly around shooting arrows into people's hearts. These arrows were soft, like magic feathers. They didn't hurt at all, but were they powerful! Anyone who was shot by Cupid would fall in love instantly.

Watch out for Cupid, Mickey! Too late. That must be why Mickey is decorating his valentine with all those hearts.

But Mickey has signed it Guess who?
Will Minnie be able to guess who sent it?

MINNIE
MOUSE

Believe it or not, there is a day on which sunshine brings bad luck. It is Groundhog Day. On February 2, people watch their favorite groundhog come out of its burrow.

If it is a cloudy day, the groundhog won't be able to see its shadow. Great! That means spring will soon be here. But if it is a sunny day, the groundhog will be so frightened by its shadow that it will run right back into its burrow. That means six more weeks of winter! Too bad, Goofy! You may have to wait a long time for that fishing trip.

February is a month for special birthdays. Every year in February, we celebrate a holiday called Presidents' Day in honor of all our presidents.

On this day, we especially remember the birthdays of two of our favorite presidents—George Washington and Abraham Lincoln.

The weather is finally getting warmer. There are days when you don't even need a coat. But the trees get new ones just the same—in shades of green, yellow, pink, and white. Spring is here.

Every spring, Grandma Duck invites Donald's nephews to see the new baby animals on her farm and to help her plant her garden.

This year the boys can't wait to get home to plant a garden of their own. First they turn over the earth to make the ground soft. Then they bury seeds in the dirt. Soon they will be picking their very first flowers and vegetables.

April Fool's Day is a day on which we love to play tricks on other people. One April Fool's Day, Morty and Ferdie played this little trick on Goofy.

APRIL FOOL!

Morty and Ferdie are having a great time decorating Easter eggs. Each egg is special. Some have stripes, others have polka dots, one has zigzags, and another has stripes and dots on it.

The Easter Bunny came last night and left baskets full of chocolate bunnies and jelly beans. The Easter Bunny loves to hide eggs in secret places. Who found a funny surprise at the Easter egg hunt?

Watch out, Grandma! The blue jay thinks that new Easter bonnet would make a great place to lay her eggs.

It's Mother's Day.
Huey, Dewey, and Louie
are planning a surprise
for Grandma Duck.

She's a wonderful grandma—and boy, can she cook! The
boys have decided to give her car a good cleaning.

See how happy Grandma Duck looks! Her car hasn't been
this clean since the last rainstorm. And as a reward, she's
baked a special apple pie. Yum!

For Father's Day, Morty and Ferdie would like to show
Mickey how much they love him. Mickey is their uncle, but he's
just like a father to them. He takes them places, and he never
really gets angry with them, even when they're a little naughty.

"You've made my day," says Mickey.
"I couldn't ask for nicer nephews!"

The summer sun is shining brightly as Donald makes breakfast for Huey, Dewey, and Louie.

"It's going to be a hot one!" says Donald. "How would you fellas like to go to the beach?"

"Yippee!" reply Huey, Dewey, and Louie. They already have their bathing suits on! "Let's go!"

"Look at those waves!" cries Huey. "How far do you think this one will take us?"

After their swim, Donald helps the boys build a sand castle.
They decorate it with beautiful shells.

"This is the best one we've ever made," says Dewey.

"I wish we could take it home with us," adds Louie.

"We'll have to settle for a picture," Donald answers. "But
we'll come back soon and make another one."

The Fourth of July is a birthday that the whole country celebrates together. Why? Because it is the birthday of the United States of America.

Instead of presents, people make lovely floats to show off in big parades. Instead of a cake and candles, fireworks light up the sky.

Every Fourth of July, Mickey has a barbecue. He
invites all his friends over for a grand outdoor feast.
When it gets dark, everyone will go to the park to
watch the fireworks from the top of a hill.

Labor Day marks the last long summer weekend before school starts. On this day, people celebrate work. They do this by not working at all!

On Labor Day, Mickey and his friends visit the county fair. At a county fair, you can see the biggest pumpkins, the reddest tomatoes, and the fattest pigs. You can even taste a delicious, prizewinning pie.

Donald's nephews love to go on rides and play the games. Sometimes they even win a prize. What a weekend of fun!

"Autumn leaves make a crunchy noise when you walk on them, don't they, Uncle Donald?"

"Yes, Huey, but I think it's time we raked them up."

"Okay, Uncle Donald, let's get started. We'll be finished in no time."

"So much for work," says Huey. "How about having some fun?"

"Don't worry, Uncle Donald. We'll clean them all up again."

It's pumpkin-picking time again, and Mickey and the gang are off to Grandma Duck's farm to pick out their pumpkins.

Grandma Duck has invited them all to go to an old-fashioned hayride. They'll sip cider, sing songs, and enjoy the crisp autumn air.

Long ago in England
people believed in ghosts, witches,
elves, goblins, and all kinds of spooky
creatures. So they dressed up in scary
costumes to protect themselves.
After all, what ghost would harm
another ghost?

On Halloween we still dress up in
costumes. Why? Because it's so much fun!

Here come Morty, Ferdie, and Donald's nephews. They want to see if they can scare Daisy.

"I've been waiting for you," says Daisy. "Can you come in to my Halloween party? We'll dunk for apples, eat some pumpkin bread, and then we'll all go trick-or-treating."

When the Pilgrims first came to America, they had nowhere to live and nowhere to buy food. So they had to build homes and grow food to eat. They were lucky that the friendly Indians helped them.

Imagine how happy the Pilgrims were to see their first crop of corn growing so high! They decided to celebrate with a big feast.

The Indians brought food and taught them how to pop corn. There was so much food, so much company, so much to be thankful for! This was the first Thanksgiving.

Many of the foods we serve today at Thanksgiving
were eaten at that first Thanksgiving: turkey, cranberries,
squash, corn, pumpkins, and yummy pies!

The first snowflakes of winter have
blanketed the ground. Morty and Ferdie can
hardly wait to try out their new sleds.
    "Last one down is a rotten egg!" yells Ferdie.

Donald is having fun making snow sculptures. Won't Daisy
be surprised to see herself standing in Donald's front yard!

Huey, Dewey, and Louie are going north with their Uncle Donald for a winter vacation. Since it is good sugaring weather, everyone is going to make maple syrup.

First they draw off sap from the trees. Then they boil the sap in kettles over a fire. Huey, Dewey, and Louie can hardly wait to pour the thick brown syrup over some snow for a delicious maple treat. Yum!

There's a special feeling in the air. Sparkling decorations, candy canes, and the sounds of carolers and sleigh bells all tell us that Christmas is on its way.

Best of all, Santa is coming! He's worked all year to make toys for the boys and girls he loves to surprise. Now his sleigh is packed. In just a short time, he'll be flying from roof to roof!

Before Santa comes, there's so much to do! There are presents to wrap, cookies to bake, and the house to dress up in its Christmas colors.

"I'll put some holly over this window," says Huey.

"I'll hang the wreath on the front door," adds Dewey helpfully.

"Let's not forget to hang our stockings by the fireplace," Louie reminds them.

Each Christmas, families decorate a Christmas tree. This is because long ago in Germany people thought that evergreens were magical. While all the other trees withered in winter, the evergreens stayed green and fresh.

"If we bring these trees inside, maybe we can share in their good luck," the people said. And that's how the tradition began.

"I love the way Christmas trees smell," says Ferdie.

"And they're great fun to decorate, too," cries Morty.

Christmas is so special, Mickey wants to share it with all his good friends. That is why they have gathered around Mickey's tree to sing their favorite Christmas songs and to share in the warm feelings that Christmas brings.